SB1054

T0066301

simple ways to praise *for piano*
Fun and Easy-to-Play Settings

Shawnee Press, Inc.
1107 17th Avenue South • Nashville, TN 37212

Visit Shawnee Press Online at www.shawneepress.com/songbooks

How to Use This Book and CD

Simple Ways to Praise for Piano brings together some of the most popular Praise & Worship songs in great sounding, yet easy-to-play settings.

Bonus! This book comes with its own Play-Along CD. This is great for rehearsal, live gatherings, worship or simply personal enjoyment as you play along.

Demonstrations of all songs are provided on the CD. You may listen to a recording of any song, as a demonstration of how it sounds when the piano is played with the track.

The included CD makes use of split tracks. What this means is the accompaniment is recorded on the left channel, and the piano on the right. Therefore, you have the capability of muting the piano by adjusting the balance on your CD player or stereo while still hearing the accompaniment, allowing you to play along.

This book indicates where the CD track begins and where the piano begins playing. The term *"Track Start"* indicates the CD start point, providing the intro for the song. In the printed music, an intro is provided for the piano in cues. The term *"Piano Start"* indicates the point in the music where the live pianist should begin playing.

Arrangements in this book can be played with or without the enclosed CD. The settings in this book are arranged in such a way as to allow for use either with play-along tracks, or as stand-alones *without* the use of tracks. If you choose to play without tracks, you may play or ignore the cued intro. Enjoy!

—The Publisher

Holy Is the Lord

Words and Music by
CHRIS TOMLIN *and* **LOUIE GIGLIO**

Strong four ♩ = 80

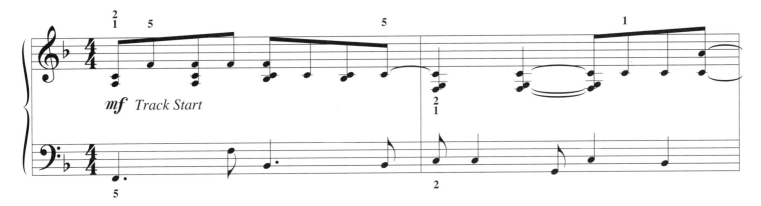

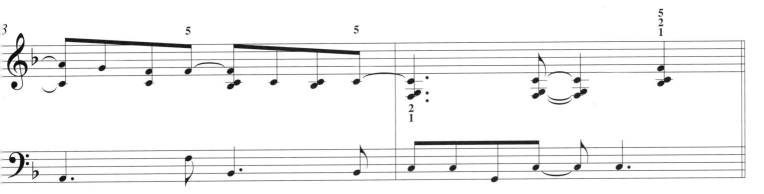

We stand and lift up our hands, for the joy

of the Lord is our strength.

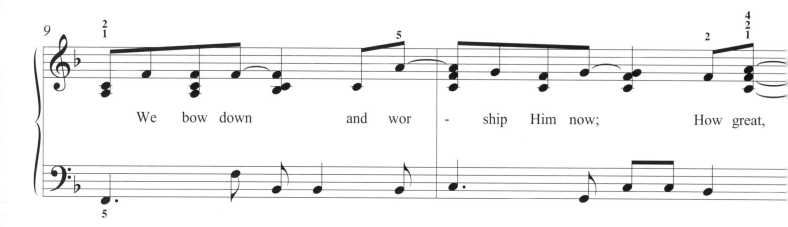

We bow down and wor - ship Him now; How great,

how awe - some is He. And to-geth - er we sing,

ev - 'ry - one

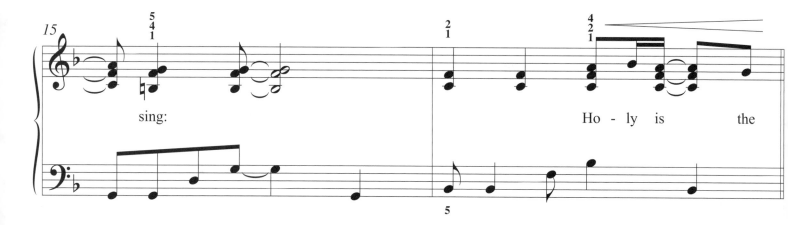

sing: Ho - ly is the

Lord God Al-might - y; The earth is filled with His glo -

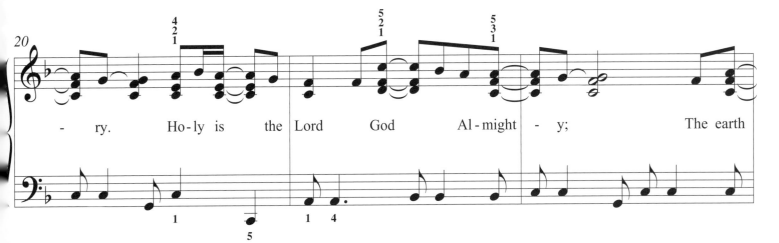

- ry. Ho-ly is the Lord God Al - might - y; The earth

Last time to Coda ⊕

is filled with His glo - ry, the earth is filled with His glo -

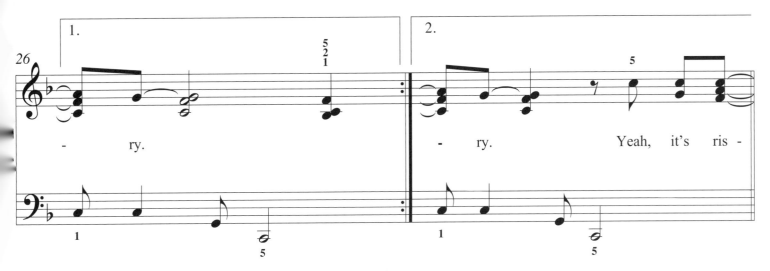

1.

- ry.

2.

- ry. Yeah, it's ris -

5

- ing up all a - round; It's the an -

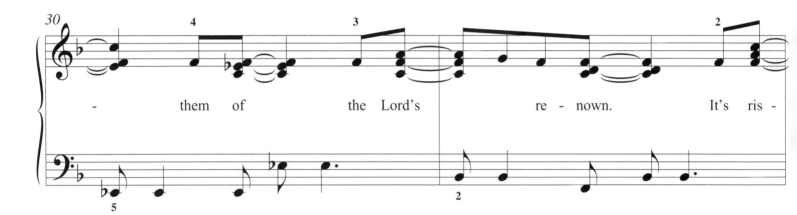

- them of the Lord's re - nown. It's ris -

building...

- ing up all a - round; It's the an -

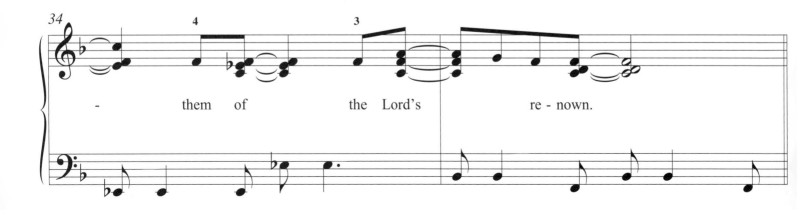

- them of the Lord's re - nown.

To - geth - er we sing, and ev - 'ry - one

D.S. al Coda 𝄋

sing: Ho - ly is the

⊕ *CODA*

- ry. the earth is filled with His glo -

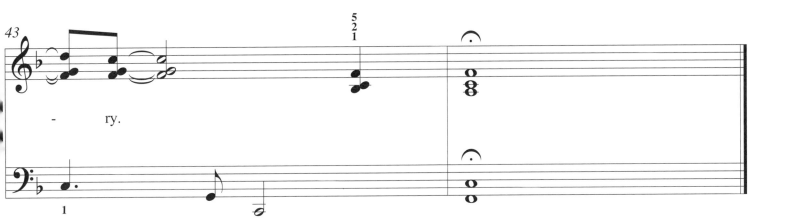

- ry.

Forever

Words and Music by
CHRIS TOMLIN

With energy ♩ = 112

mf Track Start

Piano Start

1. Give   thanks to the Lord,   our
2. might - y hand   and

God   and   King.   His   love   en - dures   for - ev -   er.
out-stretched arm   His   love   en - dures   for - ev -   er.

For He is good,   He   is a - bove all things.   His
For the life   that's   been re - born   His

love en - dures for - ev - er. Sing praise,
love en - dures for - ev - er.

sing praise. 2. With a Sing

praise, sing praise. For - ev -

- er God is faith - ful. For-ev - er God is strong. For-ev -

9

-er God is with us, for-ev - er, and ev - er, for-ev-

- er.

From the ris - ing to the set - ting sun His love en - dures for - ev-

- er. And by the grace of God we will car - ry on. His

love   en - dures   for - ev   -   er.   Sing   praise,

sing   praise..   Sing

D.S. al Coda
(to meas. 22)

praise,   sing   praise..   For - ev -

CODA

- er..

You Are My King (Amazing Love)

Words and Music by
BILLY JAMES FOOTE

Slow and worshipful ♩ = 74

12

Spir - it is with - in me be - cause You died and rose a -

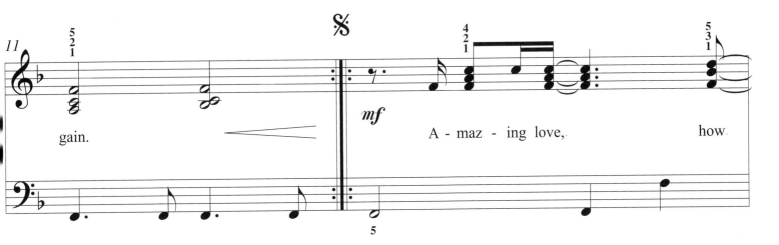

gain. *mf* A - maz - ing love, how

can it be that You, my King, would die for

me? A - maz - ing love, I

Last time to Coda ⊕
(to meas. 31)

know it's true, and it's my joy to hon - or

You. You. In all I

do, I hon - or You. You are my King. You are my

King. Je - sus, You are my King. Je - sus,

D.S. al Coda 𝄋
(to meas. 12)

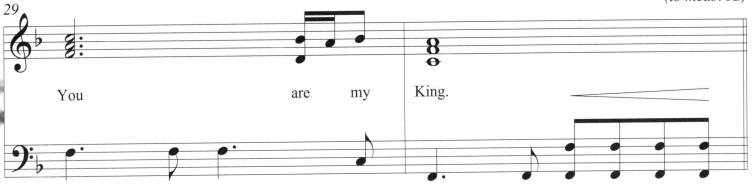

You are my King.

⊕ *CODA*

You. In all I do, I hon - or You. In all I

do, I hon - or You. *rit.*

Come, Now Is the Time to Worship

Words and Music by
BRIAN DOERKSEN

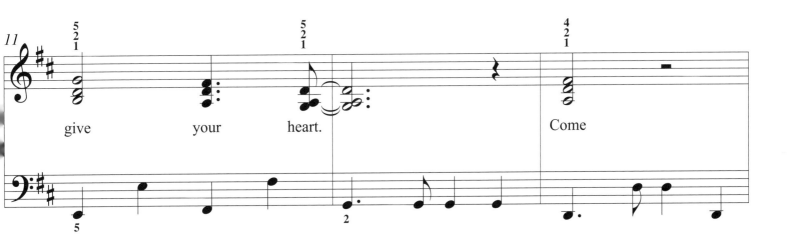

give   your   heart.   Come

just   as   you   are   to   wor   -   ship.

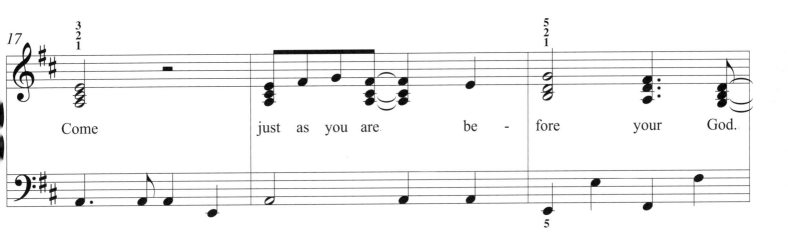

Come   just   as   you   are   be - fore   your   God.

2nd time to Coda   Come.

18

Breathe

Words and Music by
MARIE BARNETT

With much feeling ♩ = 80

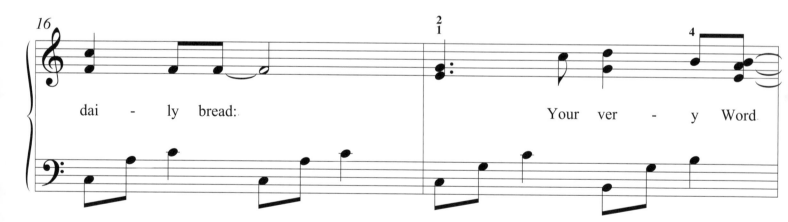

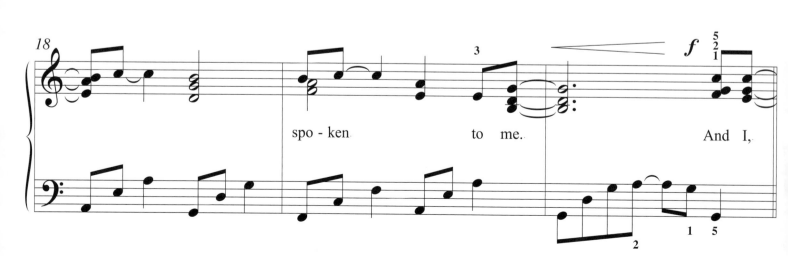

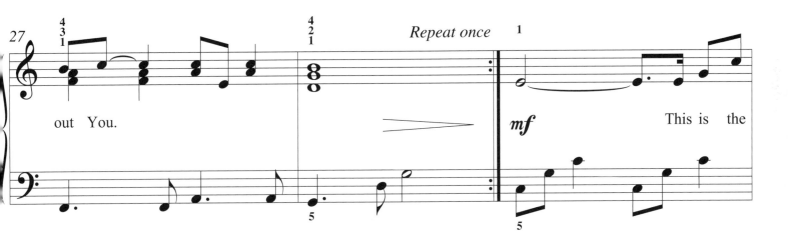

Blessed Be Your Name

Words and Music by
BETH REDMAN *and* **MATT REDMAN**

With energy ♩ = 100

be Your name.
be Your name.
be Your name.
be Your name.

Ev - 'ry bless - ing You pour out I'll turn back to

praise. When the dark - ness clos - es in, Lord,

still I will say, "Bless - ed be the

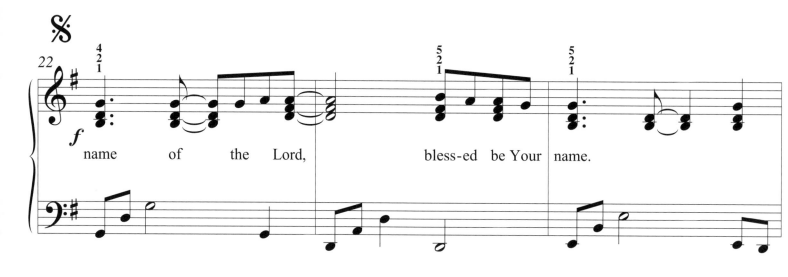

name of the Lord, bless-ed be Your name.

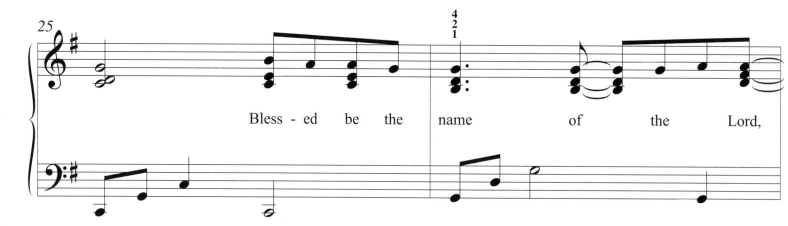

Bless - ed be the name of the Lord,

Last time to Coda ⊕
(to meas. 41)

bless - ed be Your glo - ri - ous name."

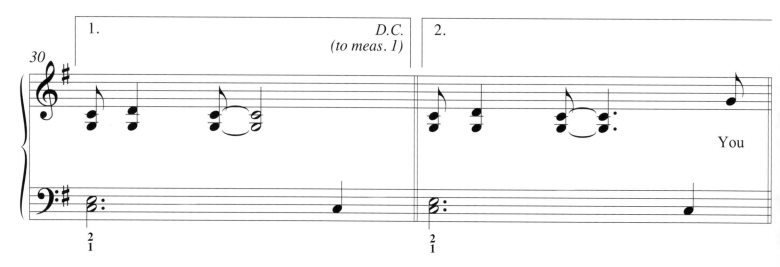

1.
D.C.
(to meas. 1)

2.

You

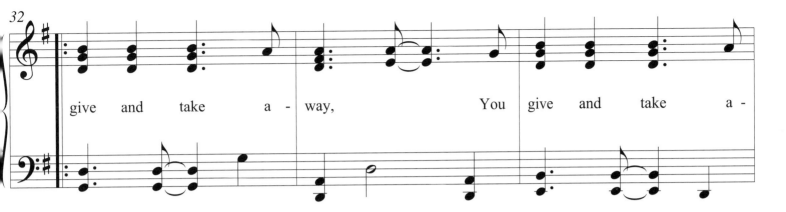

give and take a - way, You give and take a -

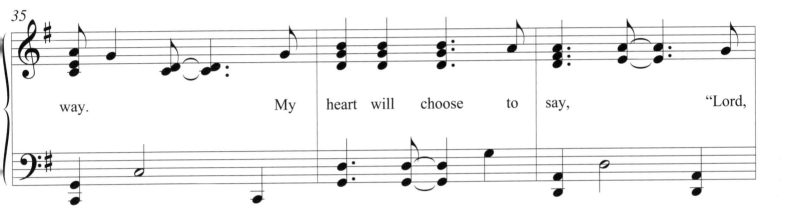

way. My heart will choose to say, "Lord,

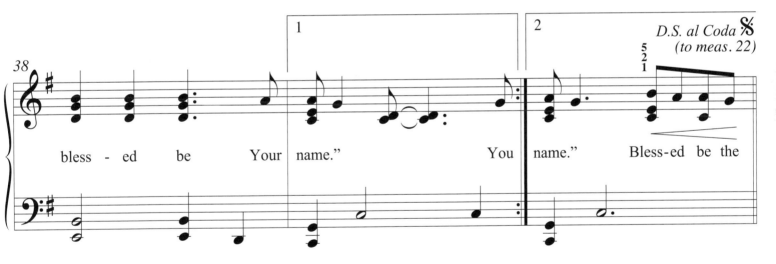

bless - ed be Your name." You name." Bless-ed be the

D.S. al Coda 𝄋
(to meas. 22)

CODA

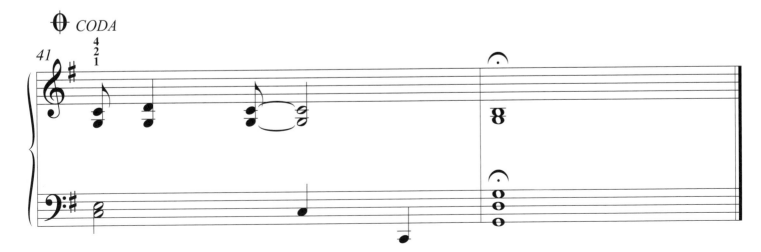

The Heart of Worship

Words and Music by
MATT REDMAN

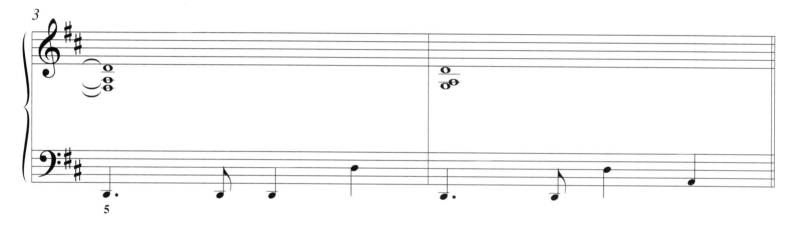

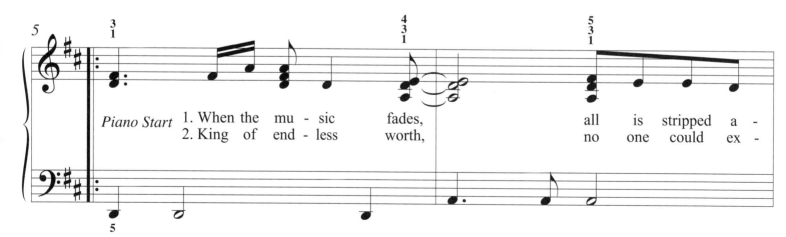

Piano Start
1. When the mu - sic fades, all is stripped a -
2. King of end - less worth, no one could ex -

all a - bout You, it's all a - bout You, Je - sus.

I'm sor - ry, Lord, for the thing I've made it, and it's

all a - bout You, it's all a - bout You, Je - sus.

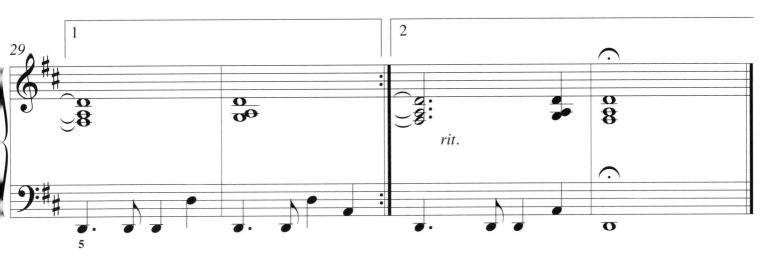

rit.

29

You Are My All in All

Words and Music by
DENNIS JERNIGAN

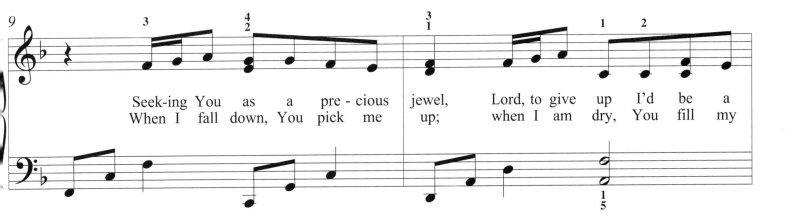

Seek-ing You as a pre - cious jewel, Lord, to give up I'd be a
When I fall down, You pick me up; when I am dry, You fill my

fool. You are my all in all.
cup. You are my all in all.

Je - sus, Lamb of God,

wor - thy is Your name.

31

Je - sus, Lamb of God,

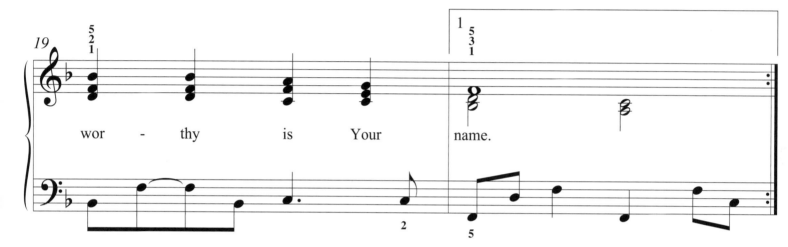

wor - thy is Your name.

name. Worthy is Your

Repeat once

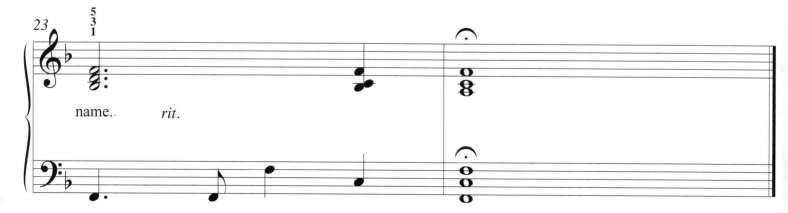

name. *rit.*

In Christ Alone

Words and Music by
STUART TOWNEND *and* **KEITH GETTY**

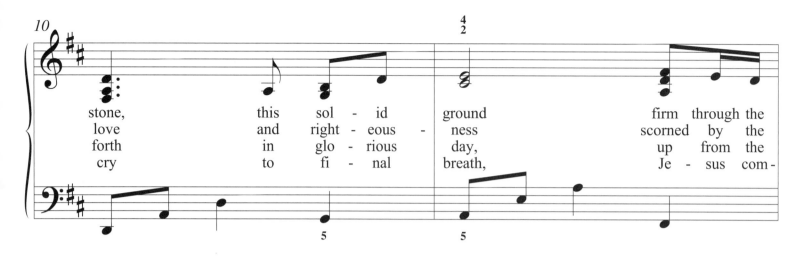

stone, this sol - id ground firm through the
love and right - eous - ness scorned by the
forth in glo - rious day, up from the
cry to fi - nal breath, Je - sus com -

fierc - est draught and storm. What heights of
ones He came to save till on of that
grave He rose a - gain. And as He
mands my des - ti - ny. No pow'r of

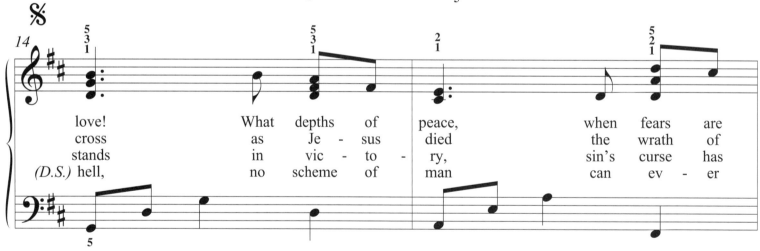

love! What depths of peace, when fears are
cross as Je - sus died the wrath of
stands in vic - to - ry, sin's curse has
(D.S.) hell, no scheme of man can ev - er

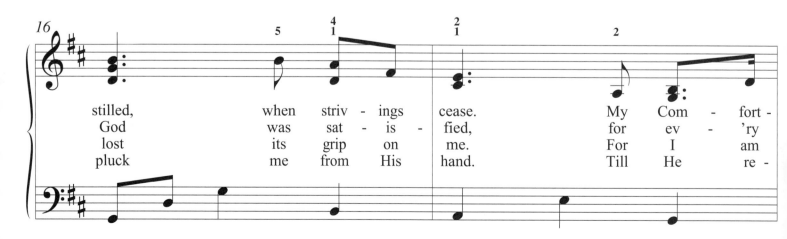

stilled, when striv - ings cease. My Com - fort -
God was sat - is - fied, for ev - 'ry
lost its grip on me. For I am
pluck me from His hand. Till He re -

34

Beautiful One

Words and Music by
TIM HUGHES

1. Won - der - ful, so won - der - ful Is Your un - fail - ing love Your cross has spok - en mer - cy o - ver me. No eye has seen, no
2. Pow - er - ful, so pow - er - ful Your glo - ry fills the skies Your might - y works dis - played for all to see. The beau - ty of Your

36

ear   has heard   No   heart   could ful - ly   know   How
ma - jes - ty   a - wakes   my heart   to   sing   How

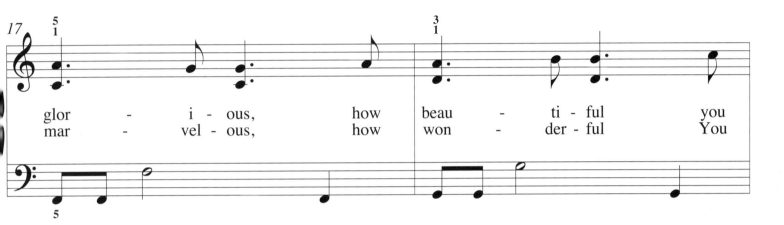

glor -   i - ous,   how beau - ti - ful   you
mar -   vel - ous,   how won - der - ful   You

1. Repeat to VERSE 2   2. To CHORUS

are!   are!   Beau - ti - ful

One   I   love,   Beau - ti - ful One   I a -

How Great Is Our God

Words and Music by
CHRIS TOMLIN, JESSE REEVES *and* **ED CASH**

clothed in maj - es - ty; Let all the earth re -
time is in His hands; Be - gin - ning and the

joice, let all the earth re - joice. He wraps
End, Be - gin - ning and the End. The God -

Him - self in light, and
- head, three in one, —

dark - ness tries to hide, and trem - bles at His
Fa - ther, Spir - it, Son, the Li - on and the

Amazing Grace (My Chains Are Gone)

Words and Music by
CHRIS TOMLIN *and* **LOUIE GIGLIO**

Steady four ♩ = 60

Piano Start

mf
Track Start

1. A -

maz - ing grace, how sweet the sound, that
2. grace that taught my heart to fear, and

saved a wretch like me. I
grace my fears re - lieved. How

once — was lost, but now I'm found, was
pre - cious did that grace ap - pear the

1. Repeat to VERSE 2

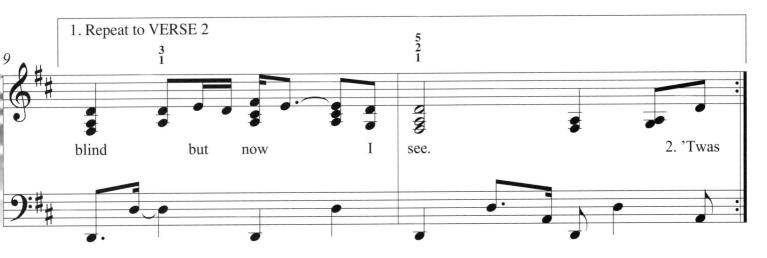

blind but now I see. 2. 'Twas

2. To CHORUS

hour I first be - lieved. My chains are

gone. I've been set free, my God, my

Sav - ior has ran - somed me. And like a flood His mer - cy reigns, un - end - ing

2nd time to Coda ⊕

love, a - maz - ing grace. 3. The

Lord has prom - ised good to me, His

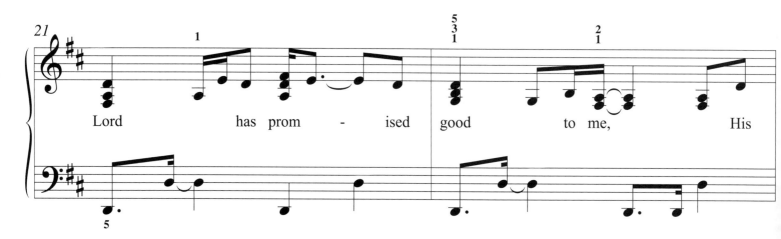

word my hope se - cures. He

will my shield and por - tion be, as

long as life en - dures.

D.S. al Coda

My chains are

⊕ *CODA*

grace.

molto rit.

Verse 4

The earth shall soon dissolve like snow,
The sun forbear to shine.
But God who called me here below,
Will be forever mine.